Illustrated by @myhollyhouse

Photography by
@georgegraiphotography

AI images by @DALL-E

The driving force behind my decision to create this guide lies in the significance of coming together, rejoicing in celebrations, and cherishing moments, whether grand or intimate, with those who hold a special place in our lives.

Hi, I'm Elizabeth Cates

In a world where children's parties often come with hefty price tags and high stress levels, I stand as a beacon of creativity and resourcefulness. With a smile as bright as my imagination, I've rewritten the rules on hosting memorable kids' celebrations without emptying your wallet. In my forthcoming book, "Your Ultimate Handbook for Kids' Parties on a Budget," I invite you into my world of thrifty yet magical gatherings.

My career took an unexpected turn when I moved to the UK from the USA and discovered my passion for organising my children's parties after starting a blog in 2017. This led me to establish "Petite Puddings" after the birth of my second child, a concept that revolutionises children's playgroups. What started as a support network for parents with social anxiety has blossomed into a playdate experience and trade show for parents to bond with their children and connect with trusted party suppliers. Not only does this serve the community, but it also supports local businesses.

@BETHBRINGSTHEBASH

Now, I am ready to share my knowledge, creativity, and empowerment with parents everywhere through this book. It's not just a guide to hosting budget-friendly children's parties; it will inspire you, demonstrating how creativity can arise from adversity.

Use this guide as a source of inspiration that shows how to be innovative even in difficult situations and how to create those picture-perfect moments without spending a fortune.

CHAPTER ONE

Budget-Savvy Bashes

Hello fellow party enthusiasts! Have you ever scrolled through Instagram and come across extravagant kiddo parties that made you wonder how you could make that magic happen without spending a fortune? Well, the good news is that you don't have to! Get ready to put on your party hats as we reveal the secrets to hosting wallet-friendly celebrations that will still be nothing short of epic.

Imagine this – my oldest child was about to turn four, and I was scrolling through Instagram, looking through photos of parties that left me feeling inspired but with a jaw-dropping price tag. It was then that I realised that throwing a legendary party did not require a money tree in your backyard. All you need is a few smart tactics, a touch of creativity, and a sprinkle of panache. Trust me, the excitement of frugal celebrations is where the true party lies!

Defining Party Success - The Real Deal

First things first, let's redefine what makes a party a smashing success. The true secret to any party is capturing candid, belly-laughing moments.

I'm all about turning party planning into a creative, wallet-friendly game. And let me tell you, it's not just about saving moolah; it's about unleashing your inner DIY diva and bonding with your little ones over crafty creations.

Picture this: you and your kids are armed with paintbrushes and a stack of cardboard, creating decorations. From funky banners to adorable homemade party hats, you'll be amazed at what a little creativity can do.

Join the #BudgetBash Party Revolution

So, here's the deal; in this book, I'm inviting you to jump aboard the budget-savvy bash bandwagon. We're going to party hard, get creative, and keep those wallets happy.

Budget-friendly parties aren't about dialling down the fun; they're about amping up, the creativity, and the connection. Let's dive into this wild world of penny-pinching parties together!
Use #BUDGETBASH and tag me in your successful-budget friendly bashes that you throw thanks to this book!

This flowchart provides a simplified overview of the budget party planning process. Depending on the complexity of the party and specific circumstances, you can expand upon each step and add more details as needed.

Party Planning Checklist

- ☑ Choose Date &Time - Start considering which locationa can be used, consider cost and weather.

- ☑ Create your guest list. Is this a whole family affair or just your child's closest friends?

- ☑ Set your budget. Concider how much you can afford to spend per person that you will invite. This will help you form your overall budget to spend.

- ☑ Allocate your budget into categories (invitations, decorations, food, entertainment and favours).

- ☑ Time for themes! The sooner you know your theme, the longer you will have to find the best prices on decorations!

- ☑ Book your venue and rentals!

- ☑ Design or purchase your invitations. (More on this later)

- ☑ Once your guest list is finalised, plan your menu or catering option.

- ☑ Plan activities and entertainment.

- ☑ Start crafting, DIY projects and make any purchases needed for your decor.

- ☑ Plan your menu, including drinks and desserts.

- ☑ Enjoy your party!

Budget Breakdown

Whether you're preparing for a big event or just trying to cut costs, it's essential to budget your money sensibly. Let's examine a sample budget of £100 as a means of distributing funds, but remember that these figures are mere estimates and can be adjusted to suit your needs. Utilise these suggestions to make the most of your funds and create a memorable #BudgetBash. As someone who's planned numerous parties and overspent in the past, I'm not a finance expert, but I've gained many valuable insights along the way.

£100 Budget Breakdown:

Decorations (£25):
- Balloons: £10
- Banners and Streamers: £5
- Tablecloths and Napkins: £5
- DIY Decor Supplies: £5

Themed Treats and Cake (£30):
- Cupcake Ingredients: £10
- Cake Mix and Frosting: £8
- Snack Ingredients (chips, popcorn, etc.): £7
- Fruit and Veggie Platter: £5

Party Favours (£20):
- Small Toys or Trinkets: £10
- Favour Bags or Boxes: £5
- Stickers or Colouring Books: £5

Activities and Games (£15):
- Craft Supplies for DIY Activities: £8
- Simple Game Supplies (bean bag toss, pin the tail, etc.): £7

Invitations and Thank You Cards (FREE)
- Printable Invitations: £3
- Thank You Cards: £2

Miscellaneous (£5):
- Disposable Plates, Cups, and Cutlery: £3
- Candles and Matches: £2

Total: £100

Budgeting Basics

Party Smart, Spend Wise

Determining Your Party Budget
Before you start decorating or sending out invites, setting a party budget that suits your financial playground is the first step. It's like planning your guest list; you've got to know your limits before sending out those invites.

Evaluating Your Finances: Know Your Numbers: Party budgeting is being real with yourself and your wallet. Take a good look at your finances. What's your monthly income, and what expenses do you already have lined up? Factor in your everyday bills, savings goals, and those unexpected rainy days.

What to Skip Out On: The Art of Prioritisation: This is where the savvy party planning kicks in. Not every line item on your list is created equal. Some are must-haves, while others are more like "nice-to-haves." So, put on your party planner hat and prioritise. That extravagant cake might need to take a backseat to a extra fun activity that gets everyone excited!

Research Costs: Don't Fly Blind
Hit up Google, call up vendors, and ask for quotes. Get a real feel for how much each element will set you back. This step is like your secret weapon; it ensures you're not caught off guard by surprise expenses.

CHAPTER

TWO

Party Logistics

Quick Reminder: These tips are essential for streamlining your party planning process.

Setting up and Decorating: Allow for ample time to set up the decorations and organise the party space. Request assistance from friends and family to ease the workload and save time.

Food Preparation: Schedule the timing of food preparation to ensure that the dishes are fresh and ready when the guests arrive. Consider preparing some items ahead of time to reduce last-minute stress.

Entertainment Schedule: Plan a schedule for party games and activities, while allowing time for breaks and transitions. Make sure the entertainment is simple, yet engaging, to keep costs low.

Managing and Coordinating RSVPs

Clear RSVP Instructions: Provide clear instructions for RSVPing on the invitations, such as a deadline and contact details, to ensure an accurate guest count.

Communication with Parents: Contact parents to confirm attendance and acquire any vital information, such as dietary restrictions or allergies to plan the menu accordingly.

Party Reminders: Dispatch reminders a few days before the party to prompt guests to remember the event and any specific details.

Clean-Up Plan: Have a plan for cleaning up after the party, including who will be responsible for specific tasks. This will make the process smoother and less stressful for everyone involved.

Thank You Notes: After the party, send thank you notes to the guests who attended. This is a thoughtful way to show your appreciation for their presence and contributions.

Finally, remember to enjoy the party! Don't get too caught up in the planning and organising that you forget to relax and have fun with your guests. With a little bit of planning and preparation, you can throw a successful and enjoyable party that everyone will remember.

Party Theme Guides

Elevating Your Budget Bash - The Ultimate Theme Guide

Get ready to transform your parties into unforgettable events without breaking the bank! We know that budgets can be tight, but that doesn't mean your celebrations have to be dull. Join us in this exciting journey where you'll learn how to throw an unforgettable bash while saving money.

Our guide begins with the most critical aspect of any party - the theme. Whether you're into elegant tea parties, superhero adventures, or a WILD safari party, we've got you covered. Say goodbye to the stress of party planning and hello to budget-friendly and enjoyable celebrations.

So, if you're ready to add some sparkle to your party hats without draining your wallet, turn the page and let me inspire you!

CHAPTER THREE

TEA-PARTY

DIY Decorations

Teacup Centerpiece's:

- Scout thrift stores for mismatched teacups and saucers. Fill them with small flowers or candles for whimsical centrepieces that evoke vintage charm.

Paper Doily Banners:

- Transform simple paper doilies into exquisite banners. String them together to create delicate garlands that add a daintiness to your tea party setting.

Vintage Teacups Candles:

- Give old teacups a second life by turning them into candles. Use melted wax and your favourite scent for a delightful centrepiece (See p.50).

Faux Flower Teapot Centerpiece

Materials Needed:
- Teapots (vintage or new)
- Faux flowers (silk or realistic materials)
- Floral foam
- Wire cutters
- Hot glue gun and glue sticks
- Greenery or foliage (optional)
- Ribbons or decorative elements (optional)
- Scissors

To create faux flower-filled teapot centrepieces, start by choosing teapots that match your party theme. Trim faux flowers to your preferred length and clean the teapots. Cut floral foam to fit inside each teapot, and secure it with a hot glue gun. Arrange the faux flowers in the foam, adding greenery if desired.

Optionally, enhance the teapots with ribbons or decorations using hot glue. Trim excess stems for a neat look. Repeat for multiple centrepieces. Place them on tables as charming focal points for your event, and consider grouping them together for a more impactful display.

Budget Hacks

Thrifted Tea Sets:

- Explore thrift stores or online marketplaces for charming, affordable tea sets. Mismatched sets can add a quaint, eclectic vibe to your tea party without denting your wallet

Thrifted Dress-Up Corner:

- Create a dress-up corner with thrifty hats, boas, and accessories. Kids can pick and choose their tea party attire without having to splurge on expensive costumes.

Rent, Don't Buy:

- If you have your heart set on vintage teacups or delicate tableware, consider renting instead of purchasing. It's a cost-effective way to achieve the look without a hefty investment.

Thrifty Eats

Homemade Scones and Jam:

- Nothing beats homemade scones. Pair them with inexpensive jams and clotted cream for an authentic touch that won't cost a fortune.

Fruit Infused Water:

- Elevate the beverage selection with DIY fruit-infused water. Use seasonal fruits for a refreshing and budget-friendly alternative to pricey drinks.

Mini Sandwiches, Maximum Savings:

- Opt for budget-friendly sandwich fillings like egg salad, cucumber, or cream cheese and chives. Cut them into dainty, bite-sized shapes for a touch of elegance.

Tea Cup Candles

Materials:

- Teacups (vintage or inexpensive)
- Candle wicks
- Soy wax flakes
- Fragrance oil (optional)
- Decorative elements (flowers, beads)

Steps:

1. Melt soy wax flakes following package instructions. Add fragrance oil if desired.
2. Attach a candle wick to the bottom of the tea cup using a small amount of melted wax.
3. Pour the melted wax into the tea cup.
4. Add decorative elements like dried flowers or beads before the wax solidifies.
5. Allow the candles to cool completely. Package each candle in a clear bag tied with a ribbon.

PIRATES
&
MERMAIDS

PIRATES & MERMAIDS
DIY Decorations

Cardboard Ship Entrance:
- Craft a grand entrance by transforming a large cardboard box into a pirate ship. Paint it in seaworthy colours, add a Jolly Roger flag, and let it set the tone for the swashbuckling adventure that awaits.

Ocean-Inspired Tablecloth:
- Use inexpensive blue plastic tablecloths to create an oceanic atmosphere. Add fishnet, seashells, and plastic marine creatures for an immersive under-the-sea vibe.

Message-in-a-Bottle:
- Roll up a message into tiny scrolls and place them in miniature plastic bottles. Seal them with twine, and guests can take them home as whimsical message-in-a-bottle keepsake to remember the party for years to come!

Thrifty Eats

Fruit Swords and Mermaid Wands:

- Create fruit swords by threading colourful fruit pieces onto skewers. For the mermaids, use star-shaped fruit like watermelon and grapes to make enchanting wands.

Ocean Potion Station:

- Set up a DIY drink station with blue punch or lemonade as the "ocean potion." Add gummy fish and use creative labels for a refreshing and budget-friendly beverage.

DIY Pirate Ship Cake:

- Transform a simple sheet cake into a pirate ship by shaping it accordingly. Decorate with chocolate sails and candy treasures for a show-stopping centrepiece that won't break the bank.

PIRATES & MERMAIDS

Budget Hacks

DIY Treasure Hunt:

- Craft a treasure hunt with DIY maps and clues. Use household items as treasure and bury them in the backyard for an exciting and cost-effective adventure.

Ocean-Themed Party Favours:

- Create budget-friendly party favours by filling small mesh bags with seashell chocolates, pirate stickers, and temporary tattoos. It's a delightful takeaway that won't plunder your pocket.

Ocean-Inspired Games:

- Plan budget-friendly games inspired by the sea. Have a "fishing pond" where kids "fish" for prizes with magnetic fishing rods, or organise a "ship race" using simple cardboard ships. These activities add excitement without straining your budget.

TEDDY-BEAR PICNIC

DIY Decorations

Teddy Bear Picnic Signs:

- Create charming signs with messages like "Welcome to the Teddy Bear Picnic" or "Bear Necessities Area." Craft these signs using cardboard, paint, or coloured paper to add a touch of whimsy to your picnic setting.

Teddy Bear Balloon Centrepiece:

- Transform stuffed teddies tied onto a pole with inflated balloons to create a floating-away teddy bear. You can create this by using teddies you already own; or look at thrifting a few extra! They also make great mini-favours if making a smaller version.

Teddy Bear Garland:

- Craft a teddy bear garland using construction paper or felt. Cut out teddy bear shapes and string them together to create an adorable garland that can be hung around the party area.

Teddy Bear Balloon Centerpeices

Materials Needed:
- Stuffed teddy bears
- Inflated balloons (helium-filled)
- Basket (optional)
- String or ribbon
- Long pole or dowel
- Hot glue gun

Gather stuffed teddy bears, either from your collection, or consider thrifting to find extra ones. Then inflate balloons with helium. Ensure they are fully inflated for a better floating effect. Attach a string or ribbon securely to each teddy bear. Tie the other end of the string to the balloon, making sure it's tightly secured.

Use a long pole or dowel as the base for your floating teddy bears. Ensure it's sturdy and can hold the weight of the balloons. Finally, use a hot glue gun to secure the teddy bears onto the pole. Arrange them in a way that gives the appearance of the teddies floating away.

TEDDY BEAR PICNIC

Thrifty Eats

Bear Paw Cupcakes:
- Decorate cupcakes to resemble bear paws by adding chocolate-covered almonds or cookies as "pads" and sliced almonds as "claws." It's a simple and charming way to tie in the bear theme.

Gummy Bear Kabobs:
- Thread colourful gummy bears onto skewers to create vibrant and tasty gummy bear kabobs. Kids can enjoy these sweet treats, and it adds a playful touch to your picnic spread.

Honey Bear Yogurt Parfaits:
- Create individual yoghurt parfaits in clear cups, layering honey-flavoured yoghurt with granola and fresh berries. Top each parfait with a small teddy bear-shaped cookie or a gummy bear for a sweet and wholesome treat.

Budget Hacks

Picnic Blanket Rental Station:
- Set up a station where kids can "rent" their picnic blankets using old blankets or fabric scraps. Let them personalize their blankets with fabric markers or paint, adding an extra layer of creativity to the party.

Nature-Inspired Party Favours:
- Encourage exploration by providing nature-inspired party favours like small potted plants, seed packets, or DIY bird feeders. It not only ties into the outdoor theme but also offers budget-friendly alternatives to traditional favours.

SUPER
HERO

DIY Decorations

Comic Book Table Runners:
- Create table runners using old comic book pages or printouts. Laminate them or use clear contact paper for durability. It's a cost-effective way to add a pop of superhero flair to your party tables.

DIY Superhero Silhouettes:
- Cut out superhero silhouettes from black construction paper or cardboard. Attach them to walls, doors, or windows to give the illusion of superheroes in action.

Pop Art Photo Frames:
- Create vibrant photo frames inspired by pop art. Use bright-coloured paper, cut-out speech bubbles, comic book-style exclamations, and superhero phrases. You can also create your own superhero-themed photo frames.

Thrifty Eats

Popcorn Power Balls:

- Create popcorn balls by shaping popcorn with a bit of honey or marshmallow. Add colourful sprinkles or edible glitter to make them sparkle with superhero power. Package them individually for easy distribution.

Caped Cupcake Cones:

- Turn ice cream cones into capes by dipping the sides in coloured icing or candy melts. Place them upside down on cupcakes to create a superhero cape effect. It's a simple and visually striking dessert that won't break the bank.

Superpowered Sandwiches:

- Use cookie cutters to transform ordinary sandwiches into superhero shapes. Whether it's a star, lightning bolt, or mask, these fun shapes add a superhero twist!

Budget Hacks

DIY Superhero Trading Cards:
- Design superhero trading cards using card stock or paper. Include fun facts about each guest and let them take their personalised trading cards home as a budget-friendly party favour.

Uncycled Superhero Masks:
- Turn old cereal boxes or coloured card stock into superhero masks. Provide elastic bands for securing them, and let the little heroes customise their masks. It's a crafty and budget-friendly addition to your superhero celebration.

DIY Superhero Capes for Chairs:
- Transform ordinary chair covers into superhero capes using coloured fabric or inexpensive felt. Attach them to the back of chairs with adhesive Velcro strips for an easy and budget-friendly decorative touch.

FARMYARD

DIY Decorations

DIY Farm Animal Balloons:

- Inflate balloons in various colours to represent farm animals. Draw simple animal faces with markers or cut-out features from construction paper and attach them to the balloons. It's a budget-friendly way to bring the farm to life.

Hay Bale Seating:

- Arrange hay bales to create rustic seating for the little farmers. Cover them with inexpensive blankets or burlap fabric for a cosy, budget-conscious seating area.

Paper Plate Farm Animals:

- Turn paper plates into adorable farm animals by painting or colouring them. Attach googly eyes and construction paper features to bring pigs, cows, and sheep to your party without breaking the bank.

Thrifty Eats

DIY Farm Animal Cookies:

- Bake animal-shaped cookies using farm animal cookie cutters. Decorate them with basic icing colours to represent cows, pigs, and chickens. It's a delicious and economical way to incorporate farm animals into your dessert spread.

Veggie Patch Crudité Platter

- Arrange colourful vegetable sticks in the shape of a garden patch. Serve them with a budget-friendly dip and label the platter as the "Veggie Patch" for a healthy snack!

Tractor Wheel Cookies:

- Bake simple round cookies and decorate them to resemble tractor wheels. Use black icing or chocolate chips to create the tire treads. It's a sweet and farm-tastic addition to your treat table.

Budget Hacks

DIY Farm Hats:

- Provide plain straw hats, which can be found at craft stores, and let the kids decorate them with adhesive farm-themed stickers. It's a cost-effective and entertaining activity that doubles as a party favour.

Seed Packet Party Favours:

- Create personalised seed packets using small envelopes and colourful construction paper. Fill them with flower or vegetable seeds and label them as "Party Seeds." It's a delightful and budget-savvy party favour that encourages a love for gardening.

DIY Plaid Tablecloths:

- Make your farm-inspired tablecloths using inexpensive plaid fabric or tablecloths. The classic plaid pattern adds a rustic touch to your party tables without expensive linens, and is great to use at your next picnic!

SAFARI PARTY

DIY Decorations

Jungle Vine Backdrop:
- Create a lush jungle backdrop using green streamers or crepe paper. Hang them from the ceiling to simulate jungle vines. Attach paper leaves cut from construction paper for added authenticity.

Cardboard Box Safari Jeeps:
- Transform cardboard boxes into safari jeeps by painting or decorating them with safari colours and patterns. Cut out circles for wheels and attach them to the boxes. Kids can "drive" their safari jeeps around the party space.

Animal Footprint Trail:
- Create a trail of animal footprints leading up to the party area using cut outs of animal paw prints or footprints. You can use construction paper or cardboard for this. It adds an element of adventure and discovery as the young explorers follow the tracks into the safari wonderland.

Thrifty Eats

Safari Snack Mix:

- Make a safari-inspired snack mix by combining animal-shaped crackers, pretzels, and dried fruit. Add a touch of sweetness with chocolate-covered raisins or candies. Package them in individual bags for easy distribution.

Fruit Safari Animals:

- Create edible safari animals using fruit slices. Arrange oranges, bananas, and grapes to form lions, elephants, and monkeys on a platter. It's a healthy and delightful addition to your safari-inspired menu.

Animal Sweet Cones:

- Create animal-inspired sweet cones. Display them in a container filled with "safari grass" made from green construction paper strips or tissue paper.

Budget Hacks

DIY Binoculars:
- Provide toilet paper rolls or cardboard tubes, and let the kids create their own binoculars using paint, markers, and string. It's a simple and cost-effective safari-themed craft that adds to the adventure.

Safari Explorer Certificates:
- Design and print safari explorer certificates using card stock or paper. Personalise them with the names of the young adventurers and present the certificates at the end of the party as a budget-friendly keepsake.

DIY Jungle Lanterns:
- Create jungle lanterns using mason jars, tissue paper, and battery-operated tea lights. Cut out animal shapes or jungle scenes from coloured tissue paper and attach them to the jars. It adds a warm and budget-friendly glow to your safari setting.

CHAPTER FOUR

Smart Swaps

Here are some smart-swap options to make your party budget-friendly without compromising on the fun!

Digital Invites

Use online platforms for easy creation and cost-effective distribution.

To make an invitation using Canva, follow these steps: sign up or log in, select a template, customize with text, images, colors, and fonts, add design elements, include event details, preview, download, and share via email, messaging apps, or social media.

Printable-Party

Use free or low-cost printable decorations and party favors available online to incorporate fun themed elements into your celebration without going over budget.

How to download free party printables on Pinterest. First create or logging in to a Pinterest account, search for specific keywords, explore pins and boards, visit websites or blogs, navigate to printables sections, browse and choose the desired printables, download them, and print them using a home printer or a local print shop. I suggests sharing the pin and respecting the terms of use specified by the creator.

Potluck Style

Transform your celebration into a potluck, letting guests contribute dishes and diversifying the menu without the burden of full catering costs

Are you planning on throwing a Halloween, Christmas or other seasonal party? Budgeting can be a major concern, but there's a simple solution. Consider organizing a potluck style party where each guest brings a dish to share with everyone. This will help you save money on food while also providing the opportunity to try out new dishes and enjoy a fun night with friends.

Thrifted Tableware

Find budget-friendly plates, cups, and utensils at thrift stores instead of buying disposable tableware, making an eco-friendly choice.

Save money on event décor that you'll likely dispose of after the event. Instead, visit your local charity shop all year round to find reusable items for future occasions. Store your finds away until the next event, and don't hesitate to display some of the unique pieces on your shelves as a reminder of the event.

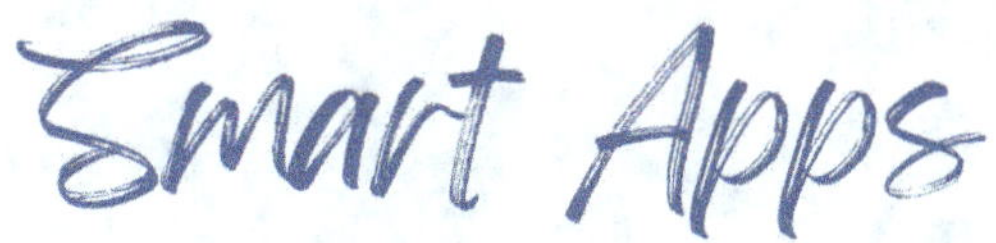

Smart Apps

Smart Apps to Simplify Your Party Planning

Tool Name	Features	Monthly Cost
Pinterest	Moodboard creation and inspiration	FREE
Canva	Built-in templates and customisable themes	Pro £9.99
Chat GPT. AI	Using ChatGPT for party planning on a budget streamlines the process by offering creative ideas, cost-saving tips, and organization guidance.	FREE
Instagram	Follow creators and children's party suppliers to gain inspiration!	FREE
Facebook	Use marketplace to find freebies, cheap decor or items you can reuse after the party!	FREE

Time Management

Allocate specific time slots for researching new tools and products to avoid getting overwhelmed. Balance staying updated on emerging trends with core responsibilities to avoid sacrificing creativity and money-saving efforts.

CHAPTER FIVE

Finding the Perfect Venue

Hiring a venue can be quite expensive, but with these tips, you could end up saving a few pounds while still getting the perfect space.

Tips for Choosing an Affordable Party Venue

At-Home Options: Explore the possibility of hosting the party at your own home or a friend or family member's residence. These options often come with cost savings and allow for more creative freedom.

Local Parks and Community Centres: Research local parks or community centres that offer affordable rental rates for event spaces. Outdoor locations can be especially budget-friendly.

Off-Peak Days and Times: Consider scheduling your party during off-peak days or times when venue rental rates are lower. Weekdays or mornings can be more budget-conscious choices.

If you decide to hire:

When choosing a venue for an event, consider the following:

Budget: Understand the full cost of renting the venue, including additional fees

Space and Capacity: Assess the space to ensure it meets attendance requirements and seating arrangements.

Facilities and Amenities: Confirm availability of required amenities and inquire about associated costs.

Contracts and Policies: Carefully review the contract and ensure you understand all terms, especially cancellation policies.

Logistics and Setup: Establish clear communication with venue staff to discuss logistics and coordinate on the day of the event.

Easy Ways to Save Money on Entertainers: Cost-Cutting Tips

Tips for Choosing an Affordable Party Entertainer

Negotiate Package Deals:
Many entertainers offer package deals that include multiple services or extended performance times at a discounted rate. When negotiating, inquire about package options to get the most value for your budget.

Seek Recommendations and Discounts:
Ask friends, family, or colleagues for recommendations on affordable entertainers they may have hired in the past. Additionally, inquire about any available discounts or promotions, especially if you are booking well in advance.

Check for Off-Peak Rates:
Some entertainers may offer lower rates for events held during off-peak days or times. If your event schedule is flexible, consider hosting your party on a day or time when entertainers are more likely to have discounted rates.

If you decide to hire:

When deciding on entertainment options for your event, keep the following factors in mind:

Audience: To ensure that the entertainment is appropriate for your audience, define your audience and theme. Make sure that the entertainment is age-appropriate.

Credentials and Experience: It's important to verify that your entertainment has been DBS checked and has experience with your audience/age group.

Reviews: Check online reviews and performance samples to get an idea of the entertainer's performance history.

Logistics and Technical Requirements: Carefully review the timings and determine what type of equipment the entertainer may require.

Contract Terms: Ensure that you abide by the contract terms and allow the entertainer to make a timely exit. Be mindful of how long you have booked the entertainer for.

Working with a Venue Decorator

Maximizing Your Options Without Overspending.

Establish a Clear Budget: Determine the budget specifically allocated for venue decoration. Having a clear budget will help you narrow down your options and find a decorator who can work within your financial constraints.

Consider All-Inclusive Packages: Some decorators offer all-inclusive packages that cover design, materials, setup, and breakdown. Inquire about these packages as they may provide better value for your budget compared to hiring separate services.
.

Explore DIY or Partial Services: If you're open to it, discuss the possibility of incorporating DIY elements or partial services. Some decorators may offer guidance or assistance for certain aspects of the decoration process, allowing you to contribute to the overall design and potentially reduce costs.

Compare Quotes from Multiple Decorators: Reach out to multiple decorators to obtain quotes for your specific requirements. Comparing quotes will give you a better understanding of the average cost in your area and help you identify decorators who offer the best value.

If you decide to hire:

When choosing a venue decorator for an event, consider the following:

Style and Aesthetic: Assess the decorator's style and aesthetic preferences. Are they versatile in adapting to different themes, or do they have a signature style?

Experience and Track Record: How much experience does the decorator have in the industry, and what is their track record for successfully transforming venues?

Communication and Collaboration: How well does the decorator communicate, and are they open to collaboration? Will they work closely with you to understand your vision and preferences?

Budget and Pricing Structure: What is the decorator's pricing structure, and how does it align with your budget? Are there any hidden costs or additional fees?

Logistical Coordination: How well can the decorator coordinate logistics with other vendors and the venue staff? Do they have experience working in various types of venues?

Booking Catering Services

Helpful Tips for Hiring a Caterer

Consider Dietary Restrictions and Preferences: Be aware of any dietary restrictions or preferences among the guests, especially if there are children with allergies or specific food preferences. A good caterer should be able to accommodate these needs.

Menu Options: Discuss menu options with the caterer, keeping in mind the preferences of the children and adults attending the party. Consider having a mix of kid-friendly and adult-friendly options.

Ask About Additional Services: Ask about additional services the caterer may offer, such as setup, clean up, and serving staff. Having a caterer who can handle these aspects can relieve you of additional responsibilities during the event.

Experience and Reputation: Look for a caterer with experience in handling events similar to yours, especially those involving children's parties. Check for reviews, testimonials, or ask for references to gauge their reputation and reliability. An experienced caterer is more likely to anticipate and handle potential challenges effectively.

If you decide to hire:

When choosing a caterer for an event, consider the following:

Insurance and Permits: Confirm that the caterer has the necessary licenses and permits to operate in your area. Also, inquire about their liability insurance to ensure you are covered in case of any unforeseen incidents.

Timeline: Establish a timeline with the caterer, including when they will arrive for setup, when the food will be served, and when they will clean up. This helps ensure that the event runs smoothly.

Menu Flexibility and Kid-Friendly Options: Ensure that the caterer is flexible in creating a menu that suits both children and adults. Verify that they can accommodate any dietary restrictions or allergies among the guests. A variety of kid-friendly options should be available to cater to the tastes of young attendees.

CHAPTER SIX

Staying Organised

Practical Organization Tips

Party Planning Calendar: Create a detailed calendar or timeline that outlines all your planning tasks, deadlines, and milestones. This will help you stay on track and avoid last-minute rushes.

Checklist Mastery: Develop a comprehensive checklist that covers everything from invitations and decorations to food and entertainment. Checking off completed tasks provides a sense of accomplishment and reduces stress.

Delegate Responsibilities: Don't hesitate to delegate tasks to willing friends or family members. Assigning specific roles and responsibilities can ease the burden on you and make the planning process more collaborative.

Timeline Checklist for Party Planning

Weeks Before the Party: Outline tasks to be completed several weeks in advance, such as sending out invitations, finalising the menu, and crafting decorations.

Days Before the Party: Detail tasks that need attention in the days leading up to the event, such as shopping for supplies, preparing food, and setting up the party space

On the Day of the Party: Provide a checklist for activities on the actual day of the party, including last-minute preparations, welcoming guests, and managing the event timeline.

Staying Stress Free

Mantras for Mindful Party Planning

Stress Reduction Strategies

Mindfulness and Relaxation: Incorporate mindfulness techniques and relaxation exercises into your daily routine to reduce stress. Deep breathing, meditation, and short breaks can work wonders.

Flexibility in Planning: Embrace flexibility in your party planning. Understand that not everything may go as planned, and that's okay. Being adaptable and going with the flow can alleviate stress.

Ask for Help: If you feel overwhelmed, don't hesitate to ask for help from friends or family members. They can assist with tasks such as setup, food preparation, or supervising activities during the party.

BUDGET WORKSHEETS

BUDGET WORKSHEET

Lets Plan a Party	BUDGET	PAID	BALANCE	DUE DATE
Venue				
Entertainer				
Cake				
Catering				
Drinks				
Invitations				
Decor				
Party Favours				
Total:				

NOTES:

BUDGET WORKSHEET

Lets Plan a Party	BUDGET	PAID	BALANCE	DUE DATE
Venue				
Entertainer				
Cake				
Catering				
Drinks				
Invitations				
Decor				
Party Favours				
Total:				

NOTES:

BUDGET WORKSHEET

Lets Plan a Party	BUDGET	PAID	BALANCE	DUE DATE
Venue				
Entertainer				
Cake				
Catering				
Drinks				
Invitations				
Decor				
Party Favours				
Total:				

NOTES:

BUDGET WORKSHEET

Lets Plan a Party	BUDGET	PAID	BALANCE	DUE DATE

NOTES:

BUDGET WORKSHEET

Lets Plan a Party	BUDGET	PAID	BALANCE	DUE DATE

NOTES:

BUDGET WORKSHEET

Lets Plan a Party	BUDGET	PAID	BALANCE	DUE DATE

NOTES:

BUDGET WORKSHEET

Lets Plan a Party	BUDGET	PAID	BALANCE	DUE DATE

NOTES:

BUDGET WORKSHEET

Lets Plan a Party	BUDGET	PAID	BALANCE	DUE DATE

NOTES:

BUDGET WORKSHEET

Lets Plan a Party	BUDGET	PAID	BALANCE	DUE DATE

NOTES:

BUDGET WORKSHEET

Lets Plan a Party	BUDGET	PAID	BALANCE	DUE DATE

NOTES:

Thank you!

When planning a budget-conscious party, it's important to remember that the true essence of any celebration lies in the love, laughter, and genuine connections that are formed during the event. The smiles on your child's face and the laughter of their friends are the most precious treasures you can ever hope to collect.

In conclusion, creating a budget-friendly children's party is not only about being economical; it's about infusing your celebration with heart and soul. It's about the joy of bringing people together, the warmth of sharing, and the magic of making memories. Embrace the journey, revel in the process, and savour every moment of your budget-friendly party, for in these memories, you've given your child a gift that will last a lifetime.

Here's to many more celebrations filled with budget-friendly fun, laughter, and the boundless joy of childhood. Let's raise a glass to celebrating the precious moments that truly matter!

Elizabeth Cates

end note review request

Please consider leaving a review on Amazon if you enjoyed reading this. Your feedback is valuable to me, and it serves as a guide for new readers who are interested in my books. Thank you for your continued support.